Rules and Laws

⇒ what are they for?

Sarah Medina

Heinemann
LIBRARY

www.heinemann.co.uk/library

Visit our website to find out more information about **Heinemann Library** books.

To order:

☎ Phone 44 (0) 1865 888066

▤ Send a fax to 44 (0) 1865 314091

▣ Visit the Heinemann Bookshop at www.heinemann.co.uk/library to browse our catalogue and order online.

First published in Great Britain by Heinemann Library, Halley Court, Jordan Hill, Oxford OX2 8EJ, part of Harcourt Education.

Heinemann is a registered trademark of Harcourt Education Ltd.

Editorial: Lucy Thunder and Helen Cannons
Design: David Poole and Kamae Design
Illustrations: Jeff Anderson
Picture Research: Rebecca Sodergren and Kay Altwegg
Production: Edward Moore

Originated by Repro Multi-Warna
Printed in China by WKT Company Limited

The paper used to print this book comes from sustainable resources.

ISBN 0 431 21001 2
08 07 06 05 04
10 9 8 7 6 5 4 3 2 1

British Library Cataloguing in Publication Data
Medina, Sarah
Rules and laws – what are they for?. – (Get wise)
306
A full catalogue record for this book is available from the British Library.

Acknowledgements
The Publishers would like to thank the following for permission to reproduce photographs: Alamy Images/Janine Wiedel p.**22**; John Birdsall pp.**21**, **28**; Bubbles p.**11**; Trevor Clifford p.**25**; Corbis pp.**10**, **14**, /Duomo p.**15**, /Tom and Dee Ann McCarthy p.**6**; Sally and Richard Greenhill p.**28**; David Hoffman p.**24**; PA Photos pp.**16**, **17**, **18**, **19**; Photofusion/Christa Stadtler p.**4**; Martin Sookias p.**12**; Tudor Photography p.**13**; John Walmsley pp.**5**, **9**, **20**; Janine Wiedel p.**23**.

Cover photograph of police and demonstrators, reproduced with permission of David Hoffman Picture Library.

Quotes and news items are taken from a variety of sources, including BBC news, BBCi Newsround and the United Nations Pachamama website.

The Publishers would like to thank John Keast, Principal Manager for Citizenship, PSHE and RE at the QCA, 1998–2003, for his assistance in the preparation of this book.

Every effort has been made to contact copyright holders of any material reproduced in this book. Any omissions will be rectified in subsequent printings if notice is given to the Publishers.

Contents

Words appearing in bold, **like this**, are explained in the Glossary.

What are rules
and laws – and
what is the point
of having them?

Rules and **laws** are part of everyone's life. We have rules at home, at school and in the community. Everyone in the country has to follow laws.

Chaos rules!

Imagine playing a game of football without rules. It would be chaos! Players would not know what they were supposed to do. They might pick up the ball with their hands and run around with it, or kick the ball into the wrong goal. No one would know who had won, or when! Rules and laws help people to know what is right and wrong. They tell us what we should do, and should not do. They help people to live, work and play together happily. Rules and laws can also help us to stay safe and healthy.

Without rules, there could be no sport because no one would know what to do!

Big trouble

Rules and laws are there for a reason. If you want to cross a busy road, you need to find a pedestrian crossing. This is where the law says that cars have to stop for you, so you can cross over safely. If the car did not stop, and you got hurt, the driver would get into serious trouble with the police. Breaking rules or the law always has **consequences** – and they are usually not very nice at all.

Doing what's right

It is up to you to do what is right! Even if you feel pressurized by other people – friends or family – to break rules or the law, you should always decide for yourself what to do. If you can, think ahead and work out where you stand. Remember – you, and only you, are directly responsible for what you think and do. And the more you get involved with making rules at home and school, the easier they will be to stick to!

🎧 It is good to express your opinions at school about important issues, such as changes in the school timetable. You can help your school to make the right rules!

Talk time

Who makes rules and laws?

ali: Adults make most rules and laws!

Lauren: Yeah, but kids can contribute, too, especially at home and school.

Tyrone: Sometimes parents and children sit down together to agree house rules.

Maribel: Like what time you have to go to bed!

Lauren: Yes, and kids can sometimes work with teachers and **school governors** to decide on rules at school.

ali: In my school, there is a school **council**, where kids get to have their say.

Maribel: It's a bit different with laws, though. In the UK, laws are made by **Members of Parliament** (MPs).

Tyrone: But people can tell MPs what they think is important.

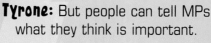

Are rules at home a good idea, or just a way for parents or carers to keep control?

L ike it or not, there are always rules at home! Sometimes they are spoken out loud, or even written down. Others are unspoken rules, which everyone seems to understand without having them spelt out.

Talk time

What kinds of rules do you have at home?

Lauren: I have to be in bed by 9 o'clock on school nights.

Tyrone: I have to do my homework straight after school, before I can go out with my friends.

ali: Me, too! And I always have to tell my parents where I'm going, and who with.

Lauren: If I get into trouble, I have to do jobs or go to bed early.

Maribel: I have to help with chores, anyway. We each have a job to do, like cleaning our rooms.

Helping out with household chores may seem boring, but it makes your home a nicer place to live in. It also frees up time for more fun activities. ➲

What's the point?

Rules at home help everyone in the family to live together peacefully. If there were no rules about how to treat each other – such as no fighting – it would be much harder to get along. If there were no safety rules – such as not leaving the fire on when you go out – there would be many more accidents in the home. If there were no rules about going out – such as telling parents or carers where you are, who you are with and for how long – the people who love you would not be able to take proper care of you.

Rule-makers

Adults have a lot of say about house rules – but children can also have their say. If everyone helps to make the rules together, it means they are easier to stick to. Some families have regular meetings, where they discuss problems and come up with solutions. This may include changing rules or making new ones. Talking things over at home is always important.

Top thoughts

'The rules for parents are but three... Love, Limit, and Let Them Be.'

(Elaine M. Ward, writer)

THINK IT THROUGH

Should children make the rules at home?

Yes. Children have to follow the rules, so they should have a say in making them.

No. Adults have more experience than children, and they know better.

What do YOU think?

School rules OK!

Are school rules necessary, or can we do without them?

If people need rules to live by in their family home, imagine how important rules are in school, where there are many more people – all with different ways of behaving. School rules help everyone in school to know what they should and should not do.

Newsflash

School rules can be for adults, too. Primary schools are making rules to stop parents behaving badly at school sporting events. One primary school in north London has a list of eight rules for parents to follow. One rule is that parents are not allowed to swear, and another one reminds them that the referee's decision is always final.

Fact Flash

In many countries, such as the UK and Australia, most schools have rules against bullying.

Rules for all

At school, safety is important. Some school rules, such as 'No bullying', help to keep people safe. Some, such as always having to wash your hands after going to the toilet, keep you healthy. Yet other rules, such as being quiet in class, and looking after school books, help you to learn better.

Talk time

What kinds of school rules do you have?

ali: In our school, we have to wear a school uniform.

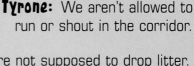

Tyrone: We aren't allowed to run or shout in the corridor.

ali: We're not supposed to drop litter.

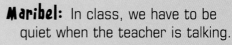

Maribel: In class, we have to be quiet when the teacher is talking.

Lauren: Yeah, and do what the teacher says.

ali: We are always told to be kind to each other, too.

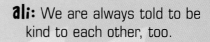

Tyrone: If you break the rules, you might get told off by the headteacher.

School rules are not just for children. Many apply to teachers and parents, too. Teachers, for example, are not allowed to hit pupils. Everyone benefits when rules make it clear what people can and cannot do.

◖ In this school, children have agreed with their teachers that they can do different things and have fun on the last day of term.

TOP TIPS

School rules are often made by **school governors**, the headteacher and other staff. But you don't have to leave it to them! Follow these top tips for helping to make rules at school:

◎ Join your school **council**.

◎ Put your ideas into a suggestion box.

◎ Discuss your views in class.

THINK IT THROUGH

Are school rules a waste of time?

Yes. Most school rules are pointless, and they just stop you doing what you like.

No. They help to make things run smoothly, so people can learn better and stay safe.

What do YOU think?

What happens when people break the rules?

Have you ever felt like breaking the rules at home or school? Sometimes, it might seem tempting. But breaking the rules always has **consequences** – and not just for other people, but for the rule-breaker, too.

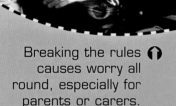

Breaking the rules causes worry all round, especially for parents or carers.

Rebel, rebel

Sometimes, young people think that rules are boring and that they are just there to spoil their fun. If they have not had a say in making the rules, they may think that they are pointless. Sometimes, they break the rules just for the sake of it, or to prove a point.

Talk time

Have you ever seen anyone breaking rules?

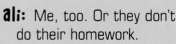

Maribel: I have seen people sneak out of school sometimes.

ali: Me, too. Or they don't do their homework.

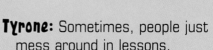

Tyrone: Sometimes, people just mess around in lessons.

Lauren: Yeah, and that makes it hard for everyone else.

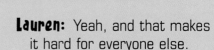

Tyrone: I have some friends who always go home late when they've been playing out.

Maribel: But then they have to stay in for the rest of the week as a punishment.

Cause and effect

Everything we do affects others – and ourselves. If you fight at school, you hurt another person, and you may be kept behind after class. If you don't listen in lessons, or don't do your homework, you will fall behind in your studies. If you scribble on school books, you ruin the books for yourself as well as for other people. If you come home late, you may be **grounded** – and lose your parents' trust. It is always best to do what is right. Ask yourself: 'What will the consequences be if I break this rule?' This will help you to make the right decision.

Newsflash

. . . .

Children who break rules about wearing school uniform may have a price to pay. In one school, flappy flares have been banned by a headteacher who thinks that kids will trip up on them. Some students have already been sent home for daring to wear the trendy trousers. In another school, kids who wear shell suits can be banned from taking part in classroom activities and given written work instead.

. . . .

These boys are spraying **graffiti** on to a wall. This spoils the area for everyone in the community – including the boys themselves.

THINK IT THROUGH

Does breaking the rules affect other people?

No. It's up to me if I want to break any rules. It has nothing to do with anyone else.

Yes. Other people suffer if you break the rules, because everything you do has an effect on someone else.

What do YOU think?

What are laws – and how are they different to rules?

Laws affect all of us, every day – including you! They affect when you go to school, what you do when you get there, the food you eat, the roads you travel on – and lots more.

Laws or rules?

Laws are similar to, but not the same, as rules. Sometimes, rules can vary – perhaps one school requires school uniform and another one does not. Laws, however, are the same for everyone. In the UK and Australia, for example, education is **compulsory** until the age of sixteen – and individual schools cannot change this. The **consequences** of breaking laws are more serious, too. People who break the law may get into serious trouble with the police.

◑ Drivers have to stop at pedestrian crossings so that people can cross the road. This law helps to keep us all safe.

A helping hand

Like rules, laws help people to know what is right and wrong, and to behave fairly towards others. They help to make sure that everyone is treated equally, and that people stay safe. Laws make crimes, such as stealing mobile phones, **illegal**. Road laws – such as having to wear a seat belt – help to prevent accidents. Animals and the **environment** are also protected by the law. For example, in countries such as the UK and Australia, it is illegal to kill or hurt **endangered** animals, such as bats and hedgehogs.

Newsflash

Animal laws in the UK may be changed to give greater protection to pets. One plan is to increase the age at which children can buy animals in pet shops, if they are not with an adult. At the moment, anyone can buy a pet, such as a cat or dog, if they are twelve or older. This may be changed to sixteen, because older kids are often more responsible and look after pets more carefully.

⟳ Smoking can kill, and so it is illegal in the UK for shopkeepers to sell cigarettes to children under the age of sixteen.

THINK IT THROUGH

Would life be better if there were no laws?

Yes. If there were not any laws, we could all do what we wanted.

No. We need laws so that people know how to treat each other properly.

What do YOU think?

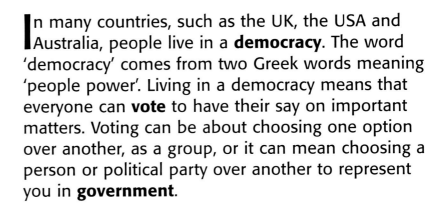

Can young
people have a
say about how
their country
is run?

In many countries, such as the UK, the USA and Australia, people live in a **democracy**. The word 'democracy' comes from two Greek words meaning 'people power'. Living in a democracy means that everyone can **vote** to have their say on important matters. Voting can be about choosing one option over another, as a group, or it can mean choosing a person or political party over another to represent you in **government**.

Your vote, your voice

Democracy is part of your life. Every time you discuss house rules with your family, vote to take a decision at school or get involved with your school **council**, you are taking part in democracy. When you are eighteen, you will be able to vote in **elections** to choose the people you want to run your community and your country.

Running your council

In many countries, people vote in elections to choose their local **councillors**. Councillors work in councils, which run different areas of the country. Every town and village belongs to a council area. Councils provide lots of services to all sorts of people. The school you go to, the library you use and the park you play in are all run by your council – and your council also organizes for your rubbish to be collected. Councils do not normally make **laws**, but they help to make sure that government laws are carried out in their area.

↩ These people are voting in a general election to choose which government should be in charge of running the country. Each person can choose what they want to happen.

Having your say

Councillors are there to listen to people's views – yours included! Even if you are too young to vote for your councillors, you can still have your say about the things that matter to you.

TOP TIPS

Follow these top tips for getting involved with what happens in your local area:

◎ Write to your councillor about an issue that is important to you.

◎ Ask if you can watch a council meeting. Perhaps you can speak at the meeting, too.

◎ See if your council has a **youth council**. If it doesn't, suggest forming one – and join up!

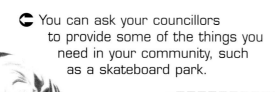

⊂ You can ask your councillors to provide some of the things you need in your community, such as a skateboard park.

Marcus' story

Young people really can have a say! Seven-year-old Marcus spoke at a meeting of his council to stop them from closing his local parks:

'The council wanted to close the small parks in my area. I found out that I was allowed to speak to all our local councillors and tell them why the parks shouldn't be closed. I said that it would mean that children would be playing on the roads and pavements, which would not be very safe. Because of my speech, the council are now rethinking their plans.'

THINK IT THROUGH

Can young people really make a difference?

Yes. Young people can influence decisions at school and in the community, by finding out what is happening, and then saying what they think about it.

No. Adults are the people who make all the decisions – after all, they can vote and have the final say.

What do YOU think?

Have you ever noticed that, every so often, your school or youth club is used as a polling station? This is where people go to **vote** in **elections**. About every five years, people vote to choose who they want to run the country in a type of election called a general election.

Political parties

Are you part of a group, such as Brownies or Cubs? People in a group usually share the same kinds of interests or ideas. In a **democracy**, political parties have members who share the same ideas about how the country should be run. These people are sometimes called politicians. Before an election, the party chooses one politician to be its leader in a particular area, such as a town. At election time, people vote for the politician they want to win.

◑ In the UK, all the MPs go and sit in **Parliament** in London. They make many important decisions that affect people's lives – for example, about what happens if someone breaks the **law**.

MPs and the PM

The person who wins most votes in a general election becomes the **Member of Parliament**, or MP, for their area. The political party with the most MPs across the whole country forms the new **government**. Their leader is called the Prime Minister. MPs are there to help people and to help to run the country, and you can tell them what you think about different issues.

🎧 Every Wednesday at 12 noon in Parliament, the British Prime Minister, such as Tony Blair shown here, answers questions from MPs about the government's plans.

Newsflash

Young people can let their government know what they think about different issues. In June 2002, a group of six schoolchildren made history by becoming the first children to give their views to MPs in Parliament. The politicians wanted to know what children thought about their **rights**. They want children to be more involved in making decisions about things that affect them.

THINK IT THROUGH

Is it good to vote?

Yes. Voting is the most important way that people can have their say. Every vote counts.

No. Voting is a waste of time. One person's vote makes no difference.

What do YOU think?

Who decides
what the law is
– and how do
they decide?

In the UK, **laws** are made in **Parliament**. There are two main sections of Parliament: the House of Commons, which has 659 **MP**s, and the House of Lords, which has 695 members. MPs in the House of Commons usually have the final say about what the law should be like, but members of both Houses discuss the law in great detail.

Making a law

Have you ever struggled to make a decision about a rule at school or home? It can take a long time for everyone to agree! Making a law is even more complicated, and it can take many months to complete the process – although laws can be rushed through quickly if they are very urgent. A law starts its life as a bill. It has to go through many stages, in both the House of Commons and the House of Lords, before it becomes a law. You can see these stages on the next page.

🎧 Bills are discussed in the House of Lords, shown here, as well in the House of Commons.

Sometimes, when bills are being discussed in Parliament, people gather outside to show what they think about the issue.

Law-making – stage by stage

This table shows the process a bill has to go through before it becomes a law.

Stage	What it means
Initial discussion	The bill is discussed with the people it may affect.
First reading	An MP introduces the bill to the House of Commons.
Second reading	MPs discuss the bill in detail, and suggest any changes.
Third reading	The changed bill is brought back to MPs for a final discussion.
House of Lords	The bill has three readings, as above, in the House of Lords.
Royal assent	The Queen formally approves the bill, which now becomes a law.

Being heard

MPs have a responsibility to listen to the views of the people who voted for them. If you want to get in touch with your MP about something you feel strongly about, you can write a letter, or talk to him or her directly in a special meeting, called a 'surgery', in your town or village. Some MPs also have 'e-surgeries', where you can ask questions or make suggestions over the Internet.

Fact Flash

In the UK and Australia, a law is also called an Act of Parliament.

Who makes sure that people do not break the law?

Parliament makes **laws** so that people know what to do and what not to do – but other people are involv with the law, too. The police help to stop people breakir the law, and catch those who do commit a crime. Judge decide what punishment to give to law-breakers.

Talk time

What kind of laws might young people break?

Maribel: Sometimes, people steal things from shops.

Lauren: Yeah, that's shoplifting. They steal things like sweets, CDs or clothes.

ali: People also steal things from other people, like mobile phones.

Lauren: Vandalism is a problem near where I live.

Tyrone: Yeah – people break the swings, and then there's nothing to play on. It's annoying!

The police are ⮕ responsible for preventing crime, as well as helping to keep us safe.

Caught in the act

When the police catch someone who has broken the law, they may take them to a police station to answer questions. This is called making an arrest. The person who has been arrested can ask for help from a **solicitor**. If the police believe that they are guilty, they will **charge** them with a crime. They will then have to go to **court**.

↻ This picture shows a case being heard in a British magistrates' court.

Going to court

The court is where it is decided whether someone has broken the law or not. The **magistrates** or judge and jury listen to all sides of the story before reaching a decision. If the person is found guilty, then he or she receives an appropriate punishment, such as paying a **fine** or doing work to help the community. For the most serious crimes, the person may have to go to prison.

THINK IT THROUGH

Do the police want to help people who get into trouble?

Yes. The police want to help young people to stay out of trouble, and they help them by talking to them and teaching them what is right and wrong.

No. All the police do is arrest people so that they stop breaking the law.

What do YOU think?

What are the consequences of breaking the law?

When someone breaks a **law**, there are **consequences** for all sorts of people. The law-breaker may be caught and punished – but the **victims** of crime are affected, too. The consequences of breaking the law are usually much more serious than for breaking rules.

Hurting others

People who have been a victim of crime often feel shocked, upset, frightened and angry. They can find it difficult to understand that somebody deliberately did something to hurt them, and they might be too scared to go out. In the UK and Australia, there are organizations that help victims of crime to get over their worries and fears (see page 31 for victim support websites).

🔊 Crime leads to punishment. These young men are having to do community service work cleaning up **graffiti** because they broke the law.

Hurting themselves

When people break the law, they hurt themselves, too. If someone drinks alcohol or takes drugs when they are too young, they may seriously damage their health. If they **vandalize** property – say, a basketball hoop in the park – they, like everyone else, will not be able to play there any more. If they get caught by the police, they will get into a lot of trouble. They may have to go to **court** and be punished.

Some people think that 🎧 damaging property does not hurt people. But this kind of crime can frighten people. It costs people money and time to sort things out.

Talk time

How would you feel if someone stole your bicycle?

Tyrone: I'd feel really upset and angry.

Maribel: Yeah, it's really annoying if someone just takes something from you.

Lauren: Especially if it was a present from someone, and something you liked a lot.

ali: I'd hate it if I couldn't use my bike whenever I wanted.

Maribel: And it is expensive to buy a new one.

Lauren: Yeah – and it feels horrible and scary that someone doesn't respect you or your stuff.

THINK IT THROUGH

Does breaking the law always have consequences for everyone involved?

Yes. Everyone gets hurt by breaking the law – even the people who do it. No one can ever feel good about law-breaking.

No. People who break the law may not always get caught, and victims of crime soon get over it, anyway.

What do YOU think?

Under pressure

Do people break rules or laws just because others around them do?

Fact Flash

Young people are more likely to break the law if they have friends who have been in trouble with the police.

Every day, people are influenced by people around them. If your friends go home early after playing out, you will probably go home on time, too. If they stay out late, you may feel under pressure to do the same thing – even though you know that it is against the rules at home. Whenever we decide what to do and what not to do, we should think about rules and **laws**. Breaking rules or the law is never a good idea, even if other people are doing it.

Peer pressure

Peer pressure is when your friends try to get you to do something you might not do otherwise. It can be hard to resist, because people usually want to 'fit in' with their friends. And so, if your friends are doing something they should not, such as skipping school or writing **graffiti**, you may feel that you have to do the same.

Media pressure

Media pressure is when newspapers and magazines, and TV programmes, influence your choices because of the things they say. They can make breaking rules or the law look normal and even exciting. That way, they can encourage you to do the wrong thing. Remember to watch out for media pressure – then you can avoid it more easily!

🎧 Don't be pushed into doing something you shouldn't or don't want to do, like drinking or smoking — it's just not worth it.

All negative?

Not all peer and media pressure is negative. Family and friends can show you positive ways to behave. News programmes often show the damage caused by crime, which can make you think twice before breaking the law.

Some games may make violence seem like fun, but violence in real life is ⓘ dangerous – and **illegal**.

Talk time

How are people pressurized into doing the wrong thing?

Lauren: If all your friends are doing something, even if it's wrong, it can be hard not to join in.

ali: Yeah, they might think you are a bit soft, and then they just make fun of you.

Tyrone: And they might not be friends with you anymore.

Maribel: It can be hard not to be part of the group.

TOP TIPS

Follow these top tips to resist peer and media pressure:

◎ Trust your own opinions, and remember that what you think is just as important as what anyone else thinks.

◎ Choose friends who share your views and interests.

THINK IT THROUGH

If a friend wants to break the law, should you try to stop them?

Yes. You shouldn't just stand by and watch without saying anything. You should tell them you think it is wrong.

No. It's up to them what they do. It is better just to tell an adult about what you have seen.

What do YOU think?

The right choice

Do you know how to make the right choice about what to do?

Everyone has a choice about how they behave. You may feel strongly that you should never break rules or the **law** – or perhaps you are not sure one way or the other. If you want to make the right choice, it will help you to think ahead about the different kinds of situations you may come across.

Getting it right

Rules and laws are there for a reason. If you think about why they are needed in a particular situation, it will be easier for you to accept them. If you help to make them, you will also feel better about them. If you ever feel tempted to break rules or the law, think about the **consequences** of your actions for other people – and yourself. If you ever feel confused, talking to a trusted adult can help you make up your mind about the right thing to do.

Top thoughts

'If you choose not to decide – you still have made a choice!'

Neil Peart, US songwriter

Remember – you ➲ don't always have to go along with the crowd! Trespassing on railway lines is against the law – and dangerous!

Have you ever...?

Have a go at this quiz to find out where you stand on breaking rules – and the law.

On a piece of scrap paper, answer 'Yes' or 'No' to each of the following questions:

- ◎ Have you ever pinched someone's sweets?
- ◎ Have you ever scribbled all over someone's work?
- ◎ Have you ever ignored your parents or carers when they told you to go to bed?
- ◎ Have you ever broken the rules when playing sport?
- ◎ Have you ever copied someone else's homework?
- ◎ Have you ever ridden your bicycle on the pavement?
- ◎ Have you ever asked someone older to buy cigarettes for you?
- ◎ Have you ever vandalized public property?
- ◎ Have you ever skipped lessons on a school day?
- ◎ Have you ever bullied anyone?

Now count up how many times you answered 'Yes' – and check out your score.

0-2 times

You find it easy to make the right choice – well done! You consider other people's feelings, and you respect them and their property.
Keep up the good work!

3-5 times

Sometimes you do the right thing and sometimes you don't. Are you being pressurized to do something you don't want to do? If so, remember that you are an individual, and that you have the **right** to make your own choices. Doing the right thing is always best.

6-10 times

You don't seem to worry about breaking rules – or the law. Stop for a minute, and think about how you would feel if someone did the same to you. Think about how your actions hurt other people. And think about how you might be hurting yourself, too.

How can you help to make decisions about rules and laws?

If you see someone throwing litter on the ground because there are no bins, do something to make a difference. Write a letter to your councillor to get them to provide more rubbish bins. ◑

Everyone has a **right** to say what they think – and to be heard. By having your say about rules and **laws** at home, at school and in the community, you can make a real contribution to the place you live. Try out some of the ideas given below and elsewhere in this book to get involved.

At home

Whenever you can, help to make house rules with your parents and carers. If you feel that a rule at home is unfair, ask to talk to your family about it. Sit down together, stay cool, and say clearly what you think and how you think things could be better. Be ready to listen as well as to talk – and to reach a decision that everyone is happy with.

At school

If you disagree with a school rule, rather than simply disobeying it, make your views known. Talk to – or join – your school **council**. Or try talking to your teacher or headteacher. If your school has a newspaper, write a letter or an article to say what you think. And ask to have a class meeting to see what others think, too.

In the community

If you feel strongly about something that is happening – or not happening – in your community, take action! Write to your local **councillor** or to your **MP** to ask them to do something about it. Get involved with groups that agree with your views. Working together with others can be very effective.

Our school RULES!

THINK IT THROUGH

Is it too difficult to speak out about things you disagree with?

Yes. Sometimes, people don't listen to you, and speaking out is scary.

No. It may be a bit scary to say what you think, but it is worth it, especially if you have thought about it carefully. If you don't speak out, you will feel even worse – and nothing will change.

What do YOU think?

Glossary

charge formally accuse someone of breaking a law

compulsory something you have to do, because rules or laws say so

consent permission

consequences results of a person's actions

council group of people (councillors) who run a local area or a school

councillor person who works for a council

court place for deciding whether or not a person is guilty of committing a crime

democracy when ordinary people have a say in how to run their country

election when people vote to make a choice about something

endangered at risk of dying out

environment our surroundings and the world we live in

fine money someone has to pay as a punishment when they have broken the law

government group of people who run a country

graffiti drawing or writing on a wall in a public place

grounded made to stay in your room or in your home for a period of time, because you have broken a rule

illegal against the law. People who do illegal things can get into trouble with the police.

law rule or set of rules that a whole community or country has to follow

lobby room in Parliament where MPs vote to make decisions

magistrate person with no formal legal training who is given the authority to enforce the law in a magistrates' court

Member of Parliament (MP) person elected to help run the country

Parliament ruling body of the UK, made up of the House of Commons and the House of Lords

right something that is fair and that you can expect

school governors volunteers who meet regularly with the headteacher to discuss and agree the way the school should be run

solicitor person who knows all about the law

vandalism/vandalize to damage public or private property on purpose

victim person who has been hurt by something that another person has done to them

vote choose one thing or person over another to get what you want or to represent you in a council or government

youth council group of young people who meet to discuss all sorts of issues, such as bullying and things to do in the community. May be part of a local council.

Check it out

Check out these books and websites to find out more about rules and laws.

Books

Citizen's Guide to Law and Order, Ivan Minnis (Heinemann Library, 2003)

DK Eyewitness Guides: Crime and Detection (Dorling Kinderseley, 1998)

Right or Wrong?, Sarah Medina (Heinemann, 2004)

Timelines: Crime and Punishment, Fiona Macdonald (Franklin Watts, 1995)

Websites

Australian government: www.nla.gov.au/oz/gov

Explore Parliament (UK): www.explore.parliament.uk

Rizer (UK government information about the law for young people): www.rizer.co.uk

School Councils UK: www.schoolcouncils.org

The Children's Legal Centre (UK): www2.essex.ac.uk/clc/default.htm

The Conservative Party (UK): www.conservatives.com

The Labour Party (UK): www.labour.org.uk

The Liberal Democrat Party (UK): www.libdems.org.uk

Australian Democrats Party: www.democrats.org.au

Australian Labor Party: www.alp.org.au

Liberal Party of Australia: www.liberal.org.au

National party of Australia: www.nationals.org.au

Victim Support (England, Wales and Northern Ireland): http://natiasso03.uuhost.uk.uu.net

Victim Support (Scotland): www.victimsupportsco.demon.co.uk/main/intro.html

Victim Support Service (Australia): www.victimsa.org/cgi-bin/index.cgi

Index

Titles in the *Get Wise* series:

Hardback   0 431 21003 9

Hardback   0 431 21004 7

Hardback   0 431 21002 0

Hardback   0 431 21000 4

Hardback   0 431 21001 2

Find out about other Heinemann library titles on our website www.heinemann.co.uk/library